Forty-
nine
syllables
on
love

Other books

Photography: History, Art, Technique
Photography - the Definitive Visual History
Photo Judging
Picture Editing
Ang's World
Photo Field Guide
Creativity for Everyone
Digital Photography Step by Step
Digital Photography Essentials
Digital Photographer's Handbook
Complete Digital Photography
Questions & Angswers
Digital Photography: an Introduction
The Complete Photographer
Digital Photography Masterclass
Fundamentals of Photography
Digital Photography Through The Year
How To Photograph Absolutely Everything
Digital Photography
Tao of Photography
Eyewitness Companion: Photography
Picture Editing
Photoshop CS For Photography
Dictionary of Photography and Digital Imaging
Digital Photography
Silver Pixels
Kiss Digital Photography
Advanced Digital Photography
Complete Digital Photography
Private Album
Digital Video Handbook
Digital Video: An Introduction

As photographer

Marco Polo Expedition
Joy of Sex
General Wade's Roads
Dorset

Forty-nine syllables on love

All text, images and book
2021 © Tom Ang

Images are from the 'Colours of White' series.

ISBN 978-0-473-55911-3

The author asserts his moral rights over this work.

Published by Nuku.Press an imprint of AngBookCo Ltd.

Introduction

One day, I started writing poems. It was after my A-level exams, when the mind is stuffed full of school-book contents that suddenly have little utility and less meaning; when music all sound too slow; and hot, long days drain into a miasma of fear, confusion, frustration and troubled dreams.

But before long, I decided that free-form poems were too permissive, much too prone to encourage emotional drivel.

I tried haiku, but found the format too tight. After a year or so of experimentation - if you can call it that - more like self-indulgent rants and stutters, it came to me that a perfect square of syllables could work.

A count of twenty-five syllables made too tight a format as that allowed only five syllables per line. And sixty-four was hard to sustain as well as being too prone to prattlingw in iambs. So I settled on forty-nine syllables: seven lines made up of seven syllables. Forty-niners.

It's of no great consequence that, as it happens, I write this some forty-nine years later. But neat is nice.

In that time, the forty-niners fell into two boxes. Loosely, and mostly for the sake of a label to put on them, those collected here are about love. The other collection is about life. The labels are about as illuminating as road names, so it's best not to put too much store by them.

At any rate, I dedicate both sets to Wendy, the glorious person who had the good sense to make me into what I am, the generosity to marry me, and has the patience to share life with me.

Tom Ang
Auckland
2021
www.tomang.com

1

Dimming the moon lost its frown
and echo-less the dawn lifts
river-hung trees their fingers
to old fugues of desires
tunelessly dissonant while
the morning stumbles indoors
without waiting for the sun.

2

Shadows tip-toe effortlessly
round your absence makes no sound
the air lies unsculpted by
your breasts long unfondled the
description on your pillow
lingers on in your perfume
like the darkness before dawn.

3

Whisper-rolled breath that should lull
a winnowing breeze throws up
themes that wave-dance in wind-waltz
flight your thoughts restively smack
at your eyes' glazing misled
by the light lapidary
sun-beams will spray hopelessly.

4

Days so sonorously smooth
that time lounges a-sloth
loving breathes the joy that lifts
the light from the possible
to the warm cadences of
caresses so age is not
time swept-by but swelling trove.

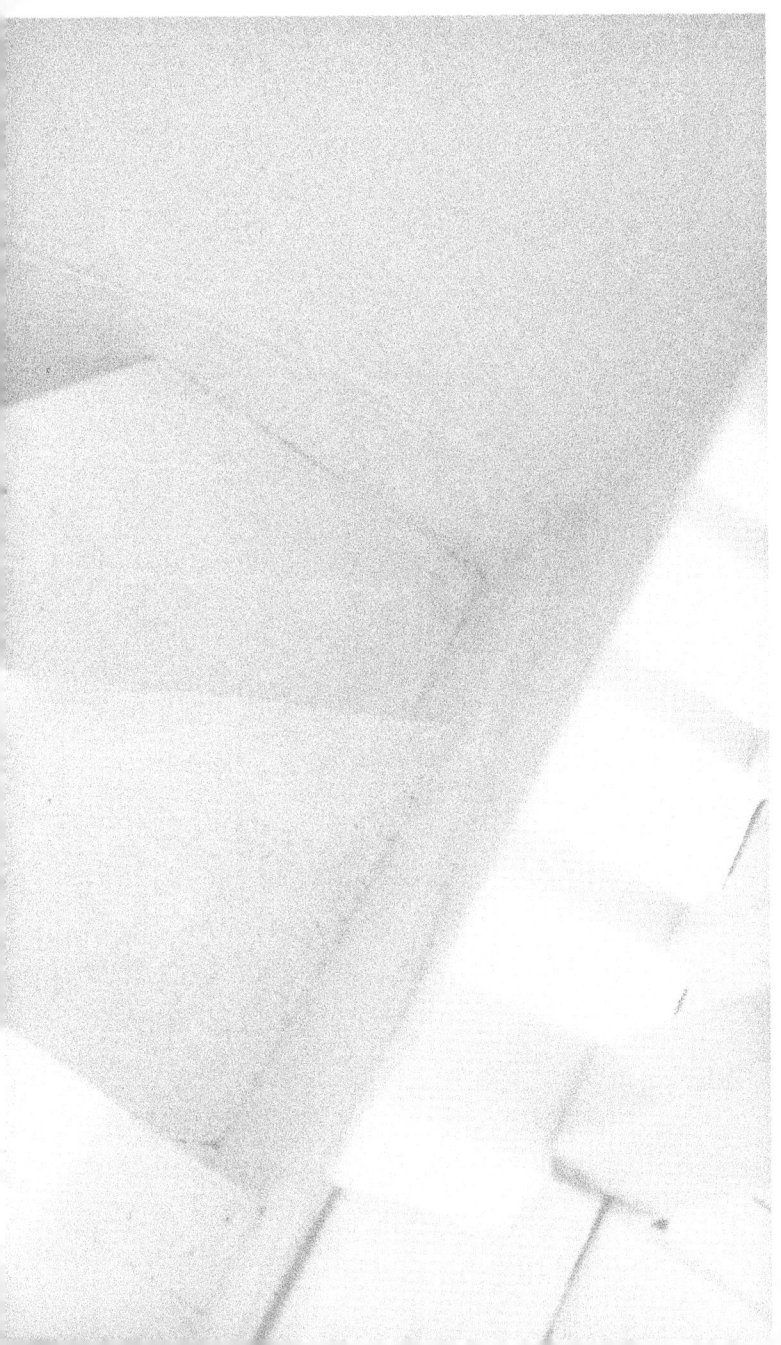

5

Graduated from far-flung
dream-energies strung out to
dry under the warmth of joy
is a power best strong when
silent thanks to which you could
as easily waltz through my
soul as lights dance in your eyes.

6

Lithesome blue ripples run cool
over the love trove's tremblings
now leafily besotted
dark beneath smooth water sheer
from my hand you soar light-wards
from dappled kisses lest I
weave long moons in loving you.

7

Loving you is each day a
genesis deft as the glide
of butterfly leaf-scrolls soft
and noiseless as the sunbeams
glide questingly not all at
at once but as shadows merge and
fruit swell sweet by degrees.

8

Less your presence shadows fall
faultlessly and move soundless
thus leaving air unsculpted
without your breasts' greeting
your breath remains folded for
absence dissolves your perfume
like darkness before dawn's light.

9

Pain is anodyne for you
the love detached from night by
soft-winged betrayals that sway
through leaves flustered by tear-fall
searching for anywhere safe
my eyes torture fearful lights
numb to wing-beats on my face.

10

Undressed mercilessly by
aged summer-fall crumpling
severally dazed to await
the torture of frosty claws
tip-toeing across your lips
glazed now in Fall's crucible
will stay chilled till dawn's poor warmth.

11

Consolable is time lost
should love be coins that do not
drop through to achieve nothing
so that your smile will dye deep
by colour-coupling to my
heart-beats with arousal's scent
their time-resistant mordant.

12

Birds gloom black along the shore
lined with their flock-spittle of
white shuttling across the loom
of wave-fall and roll as our
salty loving wefts moon-flakes
of light on the incoming
tide squirming between your toes.

13

Ours are the day-long years whose
season's octaves rise to leaf
lifting tones until gladly
blue the light-drenched breezes wave
through strands of flaxen flimsy
whose ebb is kiss withdrawn and
flow your smile opening thus.

14

Never mind that when you kissed
the swifts screamed fitfully you
left me with music shining
in my eyes a rescue from
silences you could not pierce
for I had not known fears were
hopes scrambled by too much thought.

15

Darkly susurrant run streams
under mists covert morning
wafts in milkily as lights
interleaved with whispers lift
the shadows that sarabande
cloudily with heavy sighs
spread thin by the length of night.

16

Lofted to star-heights of dark
held in a thick gyratory
embrace shivering like the
dusty dance of ancestral
ghosts in vacuum-lifted swirl
am I in enfolding sky
deep past all dreaming or pain.

17

Gaily crowned in sibilance
of sunset rays a fairy
down dance glitters across the
soft melodious leas of your
face halo-framed sailing bright
and windward into the sky
your fully perfected smile.

18

Lives flutter beautifully
near but will slip my grasp as
even faint hopes will sink all
trophies of summer's embrace
whose days spread themselves thinly
bilingual in sweet and sad
one sway from woe to cliff-edge.

19

You float a-wisp on billowed
time blithe yet watchful lest my
clammy touch mug the breezy
unfolding of ebullience
while hot blue skies hover far
from the genially absent
embrace I wait long breaths for.

20

Unpremeditated joys
bird-flung unheard to the four
winds do rob floral perfumes
from aestival bud of love-
packed hues to prove the many
ways you are beautiful span
a rainbow from peace to bliss.

21

That my joy in needing you
should drape bare feelings with words
prolegomenon to the
serious business of union
uncovers the collusion
between desire's gossamer
calligraphies and loving.

22

Filigree of trailing hair
syncope the light in gleeful
bewilderment the morning
taps the cicadas up to tune
the bell-clear skies but ignore
the slow drum of insistence
felt deeply pleasurably moist.

23

Soul's ease is love where flowers
bloom with each thought alighting
on you I may wander through
forever garden fragrant
with your scent numinous from
the after-glow of your smile
and that vermeil laugh of yours.

24

My joy in desiring you sang
from a proleptic script whose
cursive melodies ran up
my spine timed to the fireworks
of your eyes long before I
could watch their gleeful bursts float
into the jaws of darkness.

25

Memory plays with time as
willows paint the wind in strokes
from lanceolate to fumbling
while time now must wing-beat firm
into the head-winds of the
future because there is no
way to love but tirelessly.

26

Our two pink petals flutter
floundered on spider's weaving
the sun burns along the threads
as crickets screech headlong to
desiccated stillness as
pale shadows shrivel in the
breathlessness of utter heat.

27

The promise of love is a
diaphanous drift that dreams
from leaf to leaf to sun-drop
hanging by the thread of a
dawn escaped from a longing
as purple as the silence
is matte dark when you are gone.

28

A night wind-borne on salty
swells swaddles the day for dark
and light to make love and strum
up waves to arouse dry stones
with glisten of stray starry
lights playing with the moon on
its swim to black horizons.

29

Fronded shadows rustle smooth
over sleek waters willow-draped
and combed to the sky laughing
blue and bright while below the
reluctantly expanding
waves of yearnings reflect back
empty like love unanswered.

30

Reaching across space and time
your light is known by the blur
of complexity rhytmic
to butterfly erratics
whose flickering intensities
coded by cicadas are
just as recognizable.

31

You press-gang melancholy
with thoughts so unable to
feel themselves they must scrape at
the hollow of your despair
and despite the gloom made it's
all too clear how sadly your
words gaze upon each other.

32

Deliquescent is for you
the predicate of love from
damp kiss of first tenderness
to dark pools of longing for
the entry welcomed is slick
and union quenches fears which
else must cry themselves to sleep.

33

I dream in love-lost longing
spaciousness drawn by the warm
promise of light whose fondling
strokes on the atoms of your
sighs measure the years in
shadows emptying of fears
that have let go of the past.

34

Let us moon-bathe you and I
in this perfection of night
afloat in contentment some
six thousand evenings deep and
let's swim in the unruffled
unblemish of a flow eased
smooth these hundred thousand hours.

35

Light is all hollow promise
at best adorning the artful
meniscus of your lips its
reach is only atom-deep
leaving all thoughts comfortably
in the dark many glimmers
add no illumination.

36

The walnut grain of your thoughts
I love the laughter lines that
radiate italic light
converging like tracks to a
lake in your eyes are bird-song
sparkling as dappled sun-beams
scrub hard at the forest floor.

37

In your love-light do the dust
motes dance as if tickled
happy by sun-beams noiseless
as the panegyrics for
the forever must be since
the harmonics of heaven's
echoes will hear not themselves.

38

When breezes scented blue shall
freshen love-beats weakened by
betrayal then may kisses
grind up stars in a mortar
carved by waves that massaged the
bones of a land aching for
us to come to our senses.

39

Lights faltering from a thick
of stars studded to restive
emptiness pool their strength to
heart-beat the juices of flux
tempting us with tastes of art
that are deaths and births at once
like surrendering to love.

40

The root's hundred-year ache through
solid rock is an effort
of beauty computed by feel
whose tortured skeins etched by
tears twisted by degrees are
salved now by rivulets of
pleasure running off your back.

41

Let us rouse in murmur lip
to lip against such a depth
of silence its tone strokes the
underside of dawn dream-clad
it mist-glides deftly to lift
night away but their shadows'
rustling is what wakes the birds.

42

Memories are tear-streaks through
the dust of leafy hopes now
autumned to lies and hollow
endorsements but love abhors
a vacuum so must absence
be primed full if only by
a longing thickly voiceless.

43

Lying flat on the sun-deck
the day turns its back to light
fading to warm-hued love left
to inch along that tight-rope
of hope flung to time to be
that river whose thoughts run sub
rosa even to itself.

44

Lest life sail in cold waters
looking for warmth to elide
kiss with long melodies let
echo send after echo
sounding love's depth to learnt it
is only as beautiful
as surrender be total.

45

Slippery yet reliable
a sliver cut from doubt breaks
through waters stirred thickly by
winter's cold a flute breathes notes
moon-shaped in misery but
homophonous with the moans
of enraptured surrender.

46

You slip into my sleep whose
strength lay in emptiness but
now I can dive to escape
the sorrows cast dark by those
thoughts whose words slice the heads off
sunbeams like the loose flapping
of a curtain when misplaced.

47

Unwelcome reflections in
a mirror once covered by
our history's dust and lies
reveal that fears of true love
lie not in surrender to
another but in being
expected to love ourselves.

48

The catoptry of love still
muddles the picture for all
returning every gift to
source yet even with their backs
to the dark your eyes shine from
a past light-years distant to
Morse-code clues for our future.

49

Blind to insight in lightning
deaf to the wisdom in a
song-embroidered dawn faint from
stars shaken out of trees love
stalks the shadows' fall waiting
to dance on their graves 'till the
turn of night gives way to day.

www.ingramcontent.com/pod-product-compliance
Lightning Source LLC
Chambersburg PA
CBHW062028290426
44108CB00025B/2829